Garfield

THE GRUESOME TWOSOME

JIM DAVIS

RAVETTE PUBLISHING

D0505024

This edition first published by Ravette Publishing 2002.

Printed and bound for Ravette Publishing Limited
Unit 3, Tristar Centre
Star Road, Partridge Green
West Sussex RH13 8RA

by Gutenberg Press, Malta

ISBN: 1 84161 143 3

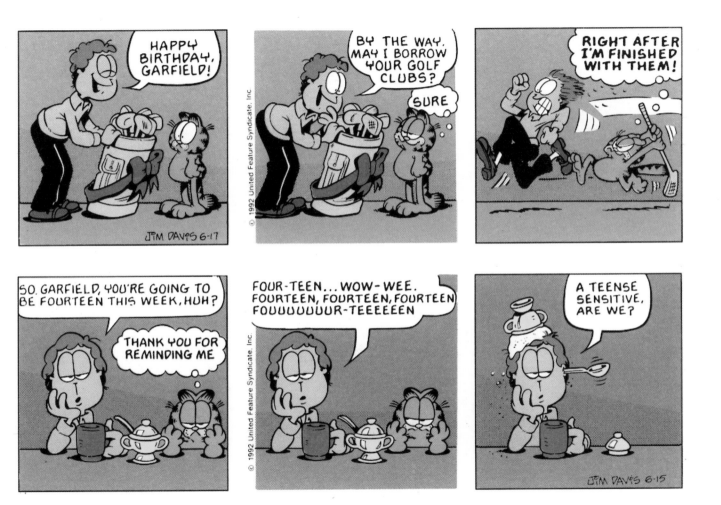

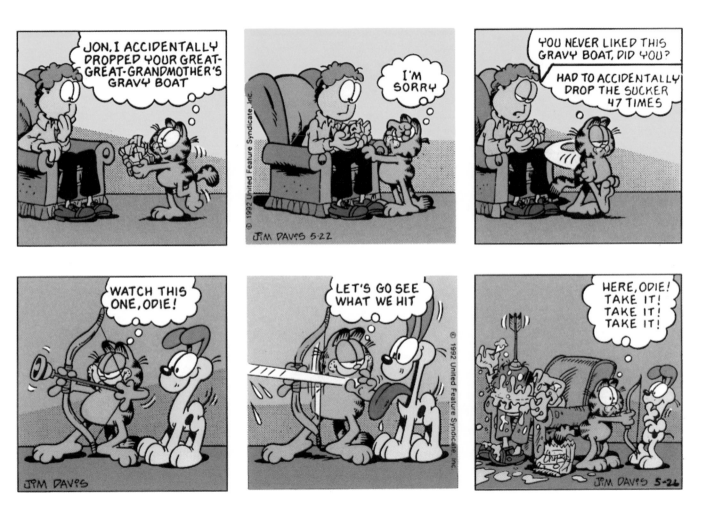

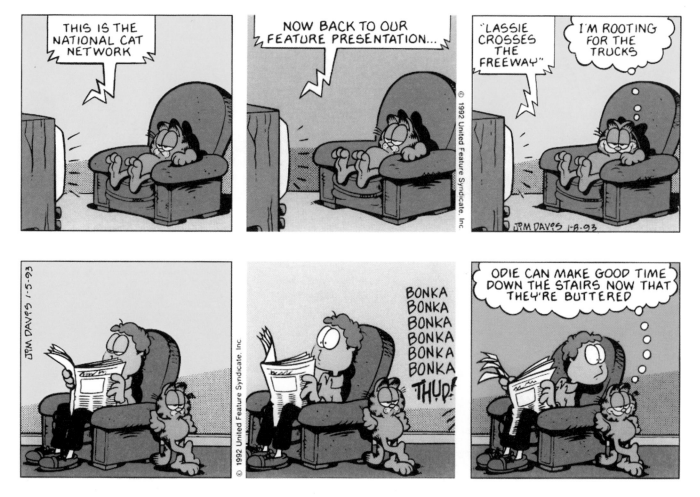

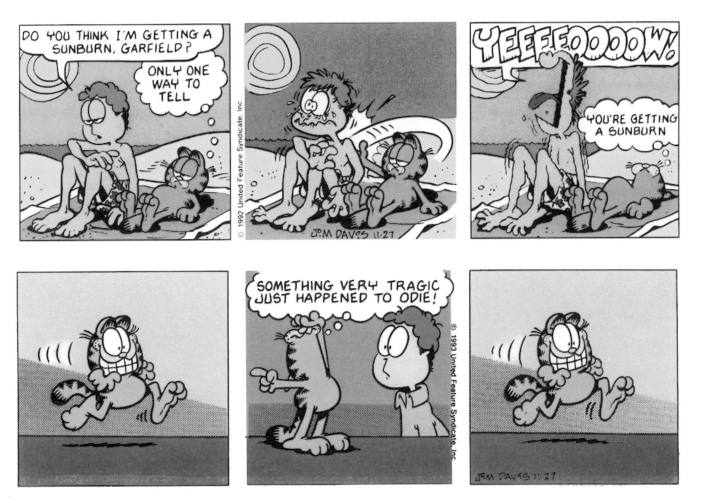

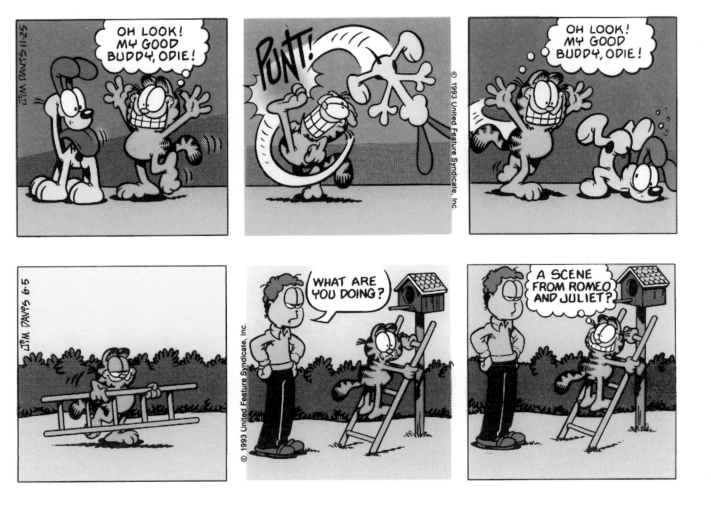

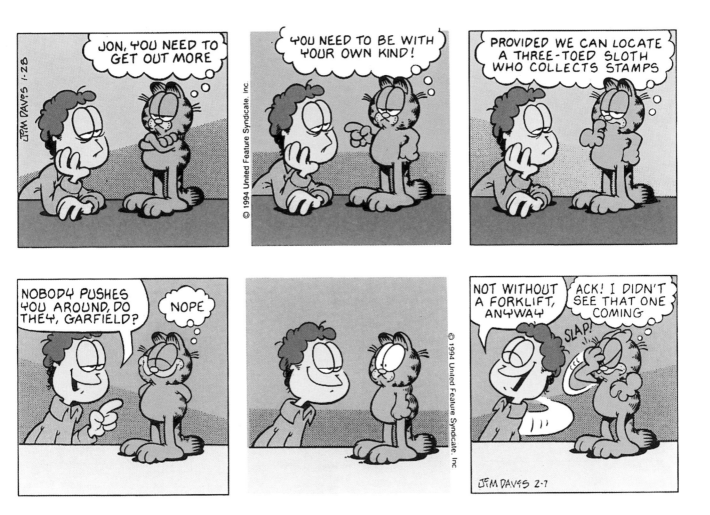

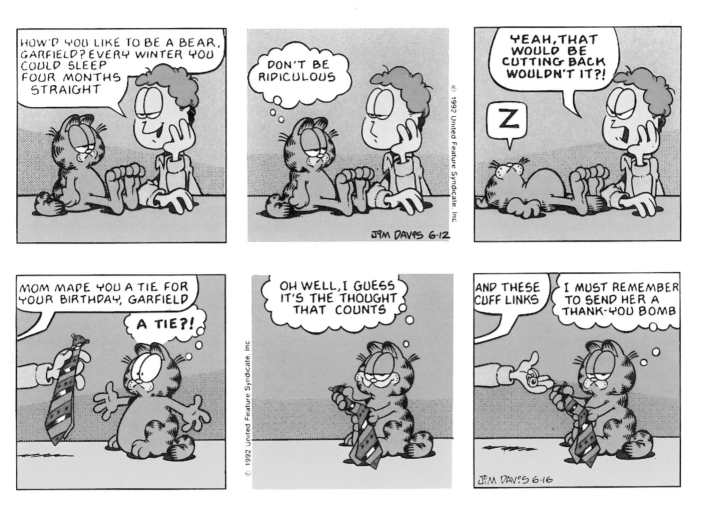

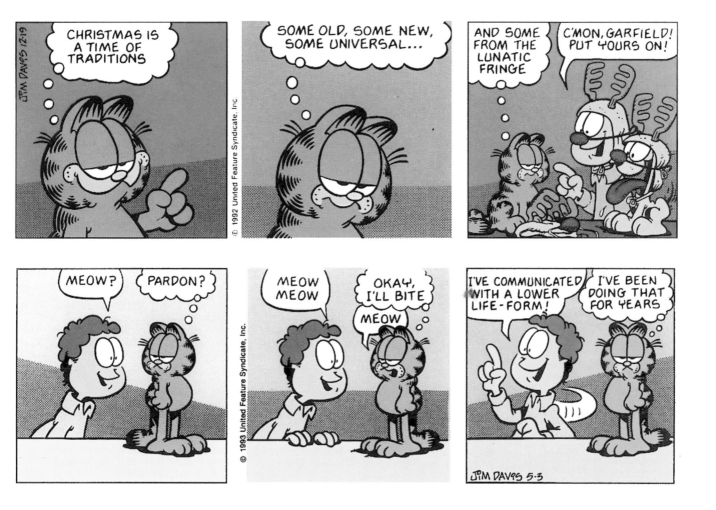

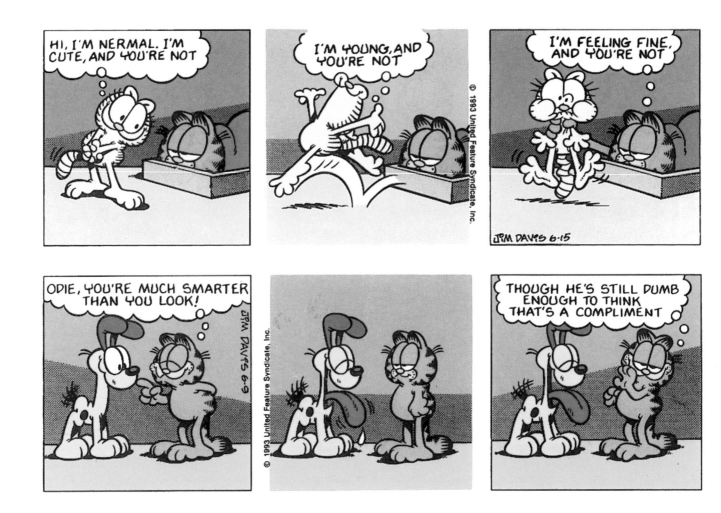

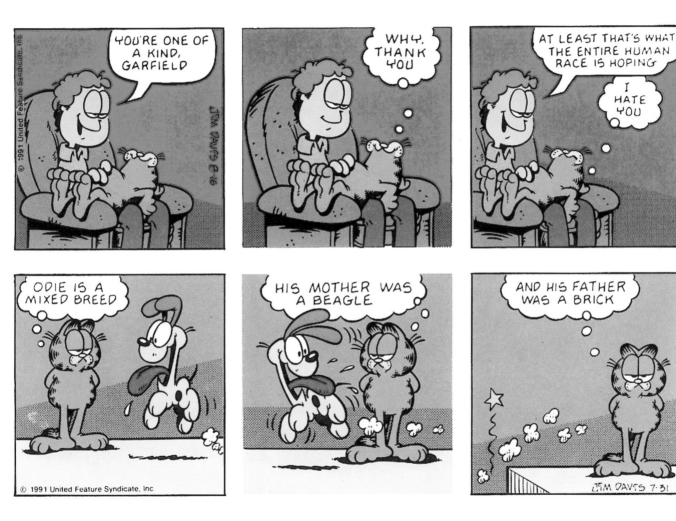

WAH-HA!
HA, HA!

© 1991 United Feature Syndicate, Inc.

BOY, HAIRCUTS
ARE DECEIVING

JIM DAVIS 4-2

TOUCH MY FOOD
AND DIE!!

© 1991 United Feature Syndicate, Inc.

OH, COME ON, JON.
YOU'RE NOT THAT
BAD OF A COOK

JIM DAVIS 3-28

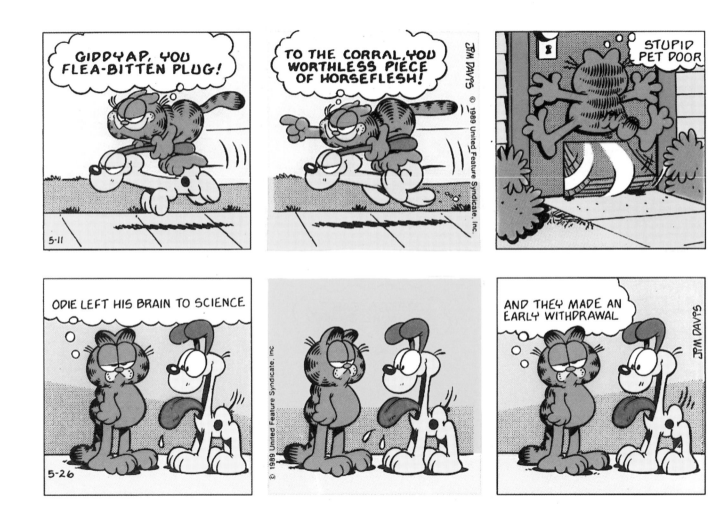

Other GARFIELD titles published by Ravette ...

Pocket Books	ISBN	Price
Bon Appetit	1 84161 038 0	£3.50
Byte Me	1 84161 009 7	£3.50
Double Trouble	1 84161 008 9	£3.50
Eat My Dust	1 84161 098 4	£3.50
Fun in the Sun	1 84161 097 6	£3.50
The Gladiator	1 85304 941 7	£3.50
Goooooal!	1 84161 037 2	£3.50
Great Impressions	1 85304 191 2	£3.50
In Training	1 85304 785 6	£3.50
The Irresistible	1 85304 940 9	£3.50
Let's Party	1 85304 906 9	£3.50
Light Of My Life	1 85304 353 2	£3.50
On The Right Track	1 85304 907 7	£3.50
Says it With Flowers	1 85304 316 8	£2.99
Shove At First Sight	1 85304 990 5	£3.50
To Eat, Or Not To Eat?	1 85304 991 3	£3.50
Wave Rebel	1 85304 317 6	£3.50
With Love From Me To You	1 85304 392 3	£3.50

New titles available February 2003

No. 45 - Pop Star	1 84161 151 4	£3.50
No. 46 - Below Par	1 84161 152 2	£3.50

Theme Books		
Behaving Badly	1 85304 892 5	£4.50
Cat Napping	1 84161 087 9	£4.50
Coffee Mornings	1 84161 086 0	£4.50
Creatures Great & Small	1 85304 998 0	£3.99
Healthy Living	1 85304 972 7	£3.99
Insults	1 85304 895 X	£3.99
Pigging Out	1 85304 893 3	£4.50
Romance	1 85304 894 1	£3.99
The Seasons	1 85304 999 9	£3.99
Successful Living	1 85304 973 5	£3.99

2-in-1 Theme Book	ISBN	Price
Out For The Couch	1 84161 144 1	£6.99
Classic Collections		
Volume One	1 85304 970 0	£5.99
Volume Two	1 85304 971 9	£5.99
Volume Three	1 85304 996 4	£5.99
Volume Four	1 85304 997 2	£5.99
Volume Five	1 84161 022 4	£5.99
Volume Six	1 84161 023 2	£5.99
Volume Seven	1 84161 088 7	£5.99
Volume Eight	1 84161 089 5	£5.99
Volume Nine	1 84161 149 2	£5.99
Volume Ten	1 84161 150 6	£5.99
Little Books		
Food 'n' Fitness	1 84161 145 X	£2.50
Laughs	1 84161 146 8	£2.50
Love 'n' Stuff	1 84161 147 6	£2.50
Wit 'n' Wisdom	1 84161 148 4	£2.50
Treasury 3	1 84161 142 5	£9.99
Treasury 2	1 84161 042 9	£9.99
Address Book (indexed)	1 85304 904 2	£4.99
21st Birthday Celebration Book	1 85304 995 6	£9.99

All Garfield books are available at your local bookshop or from the publisher at the address below. Just tick the titles required and send the form with your payment and name and address details to:-

RAVETTE PUBLISHING, Unit 3, Tristar Centre, Star Road, Partridge Green, West Sussex RH13 8RA

Prices and availability are subject to change without prior notice.

Please enclose a cheque or postal order made payable to Ravette Publishing to the value of the cover price of the book and allow the following for UK p&p:-

60p for the first book + 30p for each additional book, except Garfield Treasuries and 21st Birthday Celebration Book ... please add £3.00 per copy for p&p.